RUE DU MONT-CENIS

Fine Arts Associates, New York

MAURICE
UTRILLO

(Born 1883)

TEXT BY ALFRED WERNER

In the entire history of modern art, miracles have occurred only twice, and both times in France. Just before 1900, a poor, middle-aged civil servant, Henri Rousseau, a self-taught "Sunday painter," infused new energies and ideas into art. Shortly thereafter, a young, half-mad alcoholic of Montmartre, Maurice Utrillo, presented strange landscapes which delighted the man in the street and astonished the connoisseur. These pictures inspired many artists to re-examine their world and, instead of turning to abstraction, once again to re-create reality. Yet, except

for the miraculous element of self-preservation through art, no parallel exists between the two masters. Utrillo was the pupil of his outstanding mother, Suzanne Valadon, and a close friend of Amedeo Modigliani. Unlike Rousseau, Utrillo is not a primitive. He has been a professional painter all his life.

His is an incredible story. He might very well have ended his days, unknown to the world, as a patient in a sanatorium. Born in Paris in 1883, Utrillo is the offspring of a liaison between a teen-age model, Marie-Clémentine

CHURCH IN PROVENCE   *Museum of Modern Art, New York*

Valadon, and, so it is thought, a young amateur painter and chronic alcoholic, named Boissy. The boy's mother, an illegitimate child of peasant stock, later became the protégée of Toulouse-Lautrec, upon whose advice she changed her first name to the more elegant "Suzanne." It was Toulouse-Lautrec who introduced her to the great master Degas, who taught and encouraged her to paint.

Maurice Valadon was only a child when the Spanish writer and art critic, Miguel Utrillo, a friend of Suzanne's, in a spirit of kindness, bestowed upon him his own name. A highly neurotic youngster, Maurice was a poor student in secondary school. He was a failure, to say the least, as a bank clerk, and by the time he was eighteen had become an alcoholic and had to be temporarily committed to an asylum. It was "occupational therapy" which saved him and his hidden genius. Upon a physician's advice, Suzanne urged Maurice to take up painting as an emotional outlet through which he might regain his equilibrium. This experiment worked so well that in the past fifty years Maurice Utrillo has produced thousands of oils, gouaches, water colors, and pencil sketches, relying chiefly on his memory or the picture postcards in his possession. By 1920, he had become a legendary figure, internationally known. In 1929, the French Republic awarded him the Cross of the Legion of Honor. In his fifties he married an energetic widow, Lucie Pauwels, who managed his interests so ably that they could purchase a luxurious villa in the neighborhood of Paris where the couple is still living in grand style. It is known that, from his first confinement to an asylum to his retirement at Le Vésinet in the late thirties, Utrillo had many alcoholic relapses with self-destructive tendencies. He owes his redemption largely to the watchfulness of his mother, and then of his wife who became another gentle but firm "jailer." Even today it cannot be said that Utrillo is "a mind that found itself."

Of greater importance than his case history is the genius that alcohol was not able to destroy. Many artists and critics regard him as the century's greatest painter of urban scenes. But, in spite of his admittedly high standing, one is painfully aware of his total lack of self-criticism which permits the creation of both unbelievably inferior works and of indisputable masterpieces. Nor can one overlook the absence of intellectual concepts and the endless repetition of the same motifs in the same manner. Still, if Utrillo is only an eye, as Cézanne said about Monet, one can continue with Cézanne: "But what an eye!"

Above all, Utrillo has an eye for Montmartre—the old, picturesque, and relatively quiet artists' quarter as it existed before the First World War. He is fascinated by the sad little streets and miserable bistros of the industrial suburbs. It is true that he also painted some of the great cathedrals of France and panoramas of Brittany and Corsica, as well as a few flower pieces, but it is as the painter of the unheralded sights of the French capital that he will be known forever.

One may recognize the influence of Pissarro and Cézanne, but his solidity of composition, his gift for simplification, and his unerring sense of color relation are instinctive to him. Just as he is not a primitive, neither is he a classicist, a realist, an Impressionist, a Fauve, an Expressionist, nor even a romantic. He is a complete individualist who defies all classifications. It is customary to concentrate on the pictures of his "white period," when roughly between 1909 and 1914, white tints and shades were prominent in his work. However, the years preceding those of his "white period" yielded many fine paintings; and in the paintings of his later "colorist period" he often used bright and gay hues successfully.

Utrillo is one of the few contemporary painters whose works please sophisticated as well as simple tastes. Despite changing fashions and fluctuations of the market, his canvases bring higher and higher prices with each year—good Utrillos of the "white period" are sold for thousands of dollars. Now universally respected, he has been challenged in the courts twice and emerged victorious each time: once when American customs officials had denounced his work as dutiable products because they had been done with the aid of picture postcards; and another time when a catalogue of a London museum stated that the artist had long since perished, a victim of excessive drinking. In the second case, the squire of Le Vésinet was able to convince a British court that he was very much alive and was dividing his time between work and religious devotion.

Now seventy, Utrillo still remembers and paints the Bohemian and proletarian Paris which he roamed as a frustrated, unhappy young ruffian, yet he never visits these scenes. His life will have no tragic ending à la Van Gogh, Modigliani, or Pascin. The story's end is peace—the same peace that greets the beholder of Utrillo's transfigurations of even the most sordid places; the peace that as an old man he is now seeking with the believing soul of a child.

Commentary

COVER (PLATE ONE)
WINDMILLS OF MONTMARTRE (1949)
Collection Dr. and Mrs. Harry Bakwin, N. Y. 28″ x 35¾″

SUPERIOR IN EXECUTION TO MANY of Utrillo's recent works, *Windmills of Montmartre* delights by its fresh colors, skillfully blended to produce the most subtle textural combinations. It conjures up a rustic vista which exists only in the childhood memories of very old Parisians. There were once dozens of windmills on the exposed hill of Montmartre, their sails turning in the breeze, grinding the wheat which had been grown down below on the plain. Born and raised on La Butte, Utrillo saw the few that remained at the end of the nineteenth century as well as the two which, long before, had been converted into popular amusement places. By 1949, when he painted this picture from memory or from an old picture postcard, only one mill was still standing, Le Moulin de la Galette, famous as a night club; Le Moulin Rouge, immortalized by Toulouse-Lautrec, had given way to a movie house.

PLATE TWO
PONT NEUF (about 1908)
Carstairs Gallery, New York. 18¼″ x 20¾″

AS A YOUNG MAN UTRILLO WAS PROFOUNDLY impressed by the oils of Pissarro, which he saw at the Durand-Ruel Gallery. From them he learned to look at nature objectively and to paint it solidly, with unfaltering accuracy. In this early picture, painted prior to his famous "white period," Utrillo used the gay palette of the Impressionists; but, being a follower of Pissarro rather than Monet he did not sacrifice plasticity of form in order to capture fleeting effects of atmospheric light. Here he observes the Pont Neuf, the bridge over the Seine built in the sixteenth century in the reign of Henry III, from the left bank, the Quai des Grands Augustins. On the right the western tip of the Ile de la Cité is visible. It is a peaceful and joyous sight—the colorful barges asleep at their moorings alongside the quay; the slow-moving, moody river; the old weather-worn stone structures with their endless gradations of grey; the lush trees screening the heavy masonry of the bridge and, as a dramatic accent, the flag of France centered in the serene sky.

PLATE THREE
RUE DE LA JONQUIERE (about 1909)
Collection Alex L. Hillman, New York. 23″ x 31″

IT REQUIRED THE KEEN EYE of an artist to discover a worthwhile motif in this unglamorous street of Paris. The Rue de la Jonquière located in the 17th arrondissement (Batignolles-Monceau), and leading straight from the Avenue de St. Ouen to the Boulevard Bessières, has neither the age nor the beauty of some of the Montmartre scenes Utrillo loved to paint. The artist, however, is not concerned with beauty in the accepted sense. He would agree with a more eloquent painter of an earlier generation, John Constable, who insisted that he never had seen an ugly thing in his life, and that, however an object appears, a painter could always make it beautiful.

The year 1909, when this oil was painted, was an important one in Utrillo's life. After six years of industrious work he had achieved his own, unmistakable style. Critics and dealers usually say that his "white period" started in that year. In 1909 Louis Libaude, a dealer and writer on art, bought *Rue de la Jonquière* and several other Utrillos. Three Utrillo landscapes were exhibited at the Salon d'Automne—a great honor for a young artist. But in

1909 Utrillo also suffered a heartbreaking rebuff: his application to enroll for study at the Ecole des Beaux-Arts was rejected.

This picture, done on cardboard, as were most of Utrillo's earlier works, was painted from a window under the eaves and is reminiscent of the *perspective plongeante*—the sharp downward view—favored by Pissarro more than a decade earlier. But while Pissarro observed the scene through a window because he was too frail to work in the street, Utrillo, because of shyness and alcoholism, preferred to paint indoors in secluded attics, and eventually, to rely solely on memory and picture postcards. And while Pissarro chose for his motifs the Avenue de l'Opéra or the Boulevard des Italiens, broad and gay with throngs of people, trees, and vehicles, Valadon's moody son selected the narrow, sparsely-peopled streets of the lower classes.

The uncanny firmness of construction recalls Cézanne. Yet unlike Cézanne, Utrillo rarely defies the conventions of perspective. At the same time there is a quiet sadness such as one finds in paintings like de Chirico's *Melancholy and Mystery of a Street*, done only three years later in a similar near-geometrical, near-abstract style. But while de Chirico ends the scene at a certain point, Utrillo allows the gaze to travel far into the secrets of distance.

PLATE FOUR
RENOIR'S GARDEN (1909-10)
Collection Gregoire Tarnapol, New York. 21½″ x 31¾″

THE GREAT IMPRESSIONIST PAINTER, Auguste Renoir, though a native of Limoges (like his favorite model, Suzanne Valadon), lived in Paris from his childhood. He had many studios on Montmartre, and around 1890, at the height of his fame, he moved into the stately Château des Brouillards—the large house at the right of the picture. With him lived his wife and the two servants, Gabrielle and La Boulangère, known to us from countless portraits. Literally the "Castle of Mists," the chateau is an eighteenth-century building on the corner of Avenue Junot and Rue Girardon. From the lush garden, with its little huts and old trees, the artist, looking northward, could see the suburbs, while in the east stood the church of Sacré-Coeur, then still in construction. After a few happy years here, Renoir, plagued by arthritis, gave up his property to leave for the South. The whole section, which in Renoir's time was semi-rural, has now been completely built up. Renoir's house is now owned by the musician Marius Casadesus.

A striking feature of this painting is the dream-like vision of Sacré-Coeur, silhouetted against the grayish-blue sky and rising beyond the rather bleak garden. However much the gaudy, Romanesque-Byzantine basilica of Sacré-Coeur may lose on close inspection, seen from a distance it is highly impressive as a floating white mass of granite and marble perched on the hill of Montmartre. Thus Utrillo sees it in this painting of 1910.

PLATE FIVE
RUE DES ABBESSES (about 1910)
Collection Mr. and Mrs. John Hay Whitney, N. Y. 30″ x 41″

THE RUE DES ABBESSES, RUNNING NORTH to the Boulevard de Clichy, leads upward in the direction of the famous Montmartre Cemetery. It is named after the forty-three abbesses who, from the Middle Ages to the time of the French Revolution, ruled the convent of the Sisters of Saint-Denis in Montmartre. The towering edifice on the right side of the street is a nineteenth-century church.

In the four decades that have passed since Utrillo painted the scene nothing has changed in the general aspect of the street, save for the addition of a large advertisement, *"Buvez Coca Cola,"* recently painted on the high bare wall to the left of the church tower.

Even with the street virtually unchanged, however, the master would paint this vista today in an entirely different style. The colors would be brighter and purer, without the preponderance of zinc white. The details would be drawn more meticulously, and the people would seem less ant-like. At the same time, the feeling of definiteness and indestructibility conjured up by nearly all of Utrillo's "white period" houses would be missing. The old pictures are vigorous, and in them we see hard, commonplace structures built to be lived in. The recent pictures are pretty, but flimsy—coquettish settings of the type used by Hollywood for *An American in Paris.* When he painted *Rue des Abbesses,* one of the finest works of his "white period," the artist, who had once served as a plasterer's apprentice, still knew the substance of mortar and bricks.

Showing one of his canvases to his mother, young Maurice once asked, "Is this ugly?" Suzanne Valadon's reassuring reply was, "It can't be ugly enough!" Her answer indicated how strongly she resented that surface pleasantness which was upheld by the academies as the only acceptable beauty. In *Rue des Abbesses,* and in other canvases of the same period, Utrillo proved himself a son worthy of his mother. However different their subject matter, both artists display a masculine vigor, even brutality, of expression that will live when all *faiseurs de beauté* are forgotten.

PLATE SIX
BISTROS IN A SUBURB (about 1910)
Collection Mr. and Mrs. Peter A. Rubel, N. Y. 21¼" x 25⅝"

"BISTRO" IS AN INTERNATIONALLY USED slang word meaning "pub" or "saloon." The suburb in this instance is probably the drab and uninspiring town of Sannois just north of Paris. No tourist seeks it out, and neither Monet nor Pissarro would have wasted his brush on it. But Utrillo, then an outcast, friendless and socially inhibited, often roamed in it and in other such workers' districts. Among dealers, the term *Utrillo de bistro* was coined especially for little pictures such as this, painted in cafés or inns in exchange for a bottle of cheap wine. Today, these pictures bring huge sums at auctions.

No sunshine brightens this particular scene where sky and trees are simplified, and appear as if they had been snipped from children's drawing-books and pasted here. The houses evoke the stale aroma of neglected suburbs, the stench of poverty, and frustration.

It can be assumed that many of the paintings made by Utrillo before his "reformation" were produced under the influence of alcohol, for the artist was rarely sober when he was a denizen of Montmartre. Yet, whatever bad effects alcoholism may have had on his development as a personality, his drunken state seldom lessened his grip on the subject. His Cézannesque power to correlate sharply defined color planes in a firm architectural pattern is evident in most of his paintings.

PLATE SEVEN
RUE RAVIGNAN (about 1911)
Collection Gregoire Tarnapol, New York. 23¾" x 28¾"

THIS SHORT STREET in the Montmartre district, named for a witty nineteenth-century Jesuit preacher, played a considerable role in French literature and art during the first decade of our century. At Number 7, in a cubicle so dark that the smoky lamp had to be lit even at noon, lived the poet and painter, Max Jacob; later he moved to 13 Rue Ravignan (today the Place Emile-Goudeau), to join a crowd of young talents residing in the now famous "Bateau-Lavoir," a big sprawling house which took its name from the washing-barges in the Seine, which it faintly resembled. These men included Picasso in his "blue period," Kees van Dongen, Juan Gris, and the critic André Salmon.

Rue Ravignan offers a painter stimulating motifs. Looking down from the top, he can see Paris stretching southward as far as the Meudon hills. But Utrillo, painter of houses rather than landscape panoramas, chose to focus upon three or four edifices of banal architecture, with no historical interest. How he succeeded in eternalizing these rotting houses and shops, and how he came to invest these inanimate objects with a strange life of their own, is a miracle beyond description. The appeal in this picture depends mainly on composition and color—the well-balanced relationship of hues and geometrical forms. White and blue-black, as in most works done in the "white period," play the dominant role. Not satisfied with zinc white from the tube, Utrillo mixed it with plaster and applied it thickly with the palette knife, almost the way a mason covers bricks with plaster. He uses a multitude of "whites," and there is a moldering quality to many of them, suggesting the rottenness of aging walls superficially varnished to cover cracks and holes.

Utrillo called one of his paintings *Les Maisons Tragiques.* These are indeed tragic houses in the Rue Ravignan. Under an immobile sky (Utrillo's skies show few variations) they seem uninhabited; and yet the black rectangles painted into the walls rouse our desire to spy at the windows and discover what mysteries are hidden in the rooms.

PLATE EIGHT
FACTORIES (LES FABRIQUES) about 1911
Lewyt Collection, New York. 19½" x 28¾"

NOWHERE IN TWENTIETH-CENTURY painting can such a dreary neighborhood as this be found except on the canvases of the American painter, Ben Shahn. But while Shahn's work is always concerned with social protest, *Les Fabriques* conjures up no visions of the work-slaves in this factory neighborhood. Here we have a study in color and form relations with an unorthodox use of perspective unusual with Utrillo. In 1911, no one else had cared, or even dared, to fill a picture with little more than solid rectangles of color. Parallel to the Fauves and the Cubists, but without program, Utrillo had begun to reduce houses, chimneys, and windows to geometrical statements, to arrangements of horizontal and vertical lines, filling in the forms with color.

Drama is brought into this rigid, two-dimensional arrangement by the striking inscriptions *Hotel* and *Vins Liqueurs* on the left, and the unexpected irregularity of the tree on the right. That a tree could grow in such a bleak and dreary neighborhood as this is ironic, and one grasps the irony of the gay red and yellow on the dismal factory walls. These reds and yellows create surrealistic effects as does the frightening black of the windows, rendered particularly bleak by the light color surrounding them. Here, under an unbelievably pleasant and traditional sky, the absence of human beings is even more haunting than in *Rue Ravignan* (plate seven).

It was indeed an unhappy soul who avoided the beautiful corners of Paris and sought out this combination of bare, dirty walls to serve as a background for his abysmal struggle with the invisible forces of darkness!

PLATE NINE
PLACE DU TERTRE (about 1911-12)
Tate Gallery, London. 19⅞" x 28¾"

UTRILLO WAS A NATIVE OF THE BUTTE, the steep hill of Montmartre which rises five hundred feet above the noisy boulevards. He has frequently painted the Place du Tertre, originally the main square of what had been an independent village outside of Paris. Until the first World War, artists lived on the Butte in dozens of small courtyard studios hidden in the tiny streets which fork off from the square. At the bare, scrubbed tables of the little bistros, such young artists as Picasso, Vlaminck, Derain, Modigliani, and Utrillo ate and drank. Later, as up-to-date bars and restaurants were established to attract swarms of tourists, the artists left their lost paradise to move to Montparnasse on the left bank of the Seine. Utrillo, however, remained in Montmartre a long while. Even now, safely removed from the alcoholic dangers of the Butte, he still likes to recall its quaint old buildings and winding streets.

This picture shows the square—named for a French explorer who died in Africa—in late fall or winter. Utrillo's melancholy soul preferred the desolate seasons to the months of warmth and bloom. He liked low-keyed colors and the lacy patterns of bare boughs. In this picture, as in many others, he is fascinated by the lettering on stores and buildings. These letters, over-large and stiff, are introduced for their decorative effect as well as for what they suggest—*Vins, Liqueurs, Restaurant, Epicerie, Patisserie, Tabac.*

Notwithstanding all *mise en scène* and make-believe for the tourist's sake, Place du Tertre has changed so much in the last three or four decades that this painting has now historical as well as artistic value. However the future evaluates him as an artist, Utrillo will live as an ardent chronicler of a vanished Montmartre.

PLATE TEN
NOTRE-DAME DE CLIGNANCOURT (about 1912)
Collection Mrs. Camille Dreyfus, New York. 24″ x 32′

UTRILLO, A FERVENT CATHOLIC, has painted dozens of French churches, ranging from such striking monuments of the Middle Ages as the cathedrals of Chartres and Rheims to the new and less interesting churches of the countryside. Notre-Dame de Clignancourt, built by Lequeux in 1859-1863, is not even mentioned by Baedeker. Constructed on what was then farmland, this church is in Romanesque style, in the form of a Latin cross of unusual length, 300 feet long and 100 feet broad. Utrillo painted this church many times and from many angles. In this version, the streets are covered with snow, the spectator is standing on the Place Jules Joffrin looking northward towards the suburbs, with the Rue Hermel to his right, and the Rue du Mont-Cenis to his left.

Here, in this typical product of Utrillo's *manière blanche*, the artist has once again proved his ability to "clothe in splendor all that the casual eye of the passer-by neglects," as Adolphe Tabarant has said. It is interesting to imagine how Monet would have painted this church. In all likelihood, he would have painted only part of the church, dissolving the solid façade into a dazzling miracle of atmospheric vibrancies, re-creating the layers of air between the church and himself rather than the façade, until all feeling that it was made of stone would be lost.

Utrillo, however, has never been interested in the phenomenon of light as such, nor in the shadows resulting from the sun's position. He has a feeling for three dimensionality, for construction, for clarity of statement. One might say that just as Renoir had a sense of flesh, so Utrillo has a sense of stone. It is a curious fact, that Utrillo, even at the time when he was an alcoholic, never allowed doubt or disorder to mar the strict construction of his paintings. Within the traditional framework of an utterly conventional and symmetrical composition, the noble simplicity of the central motif is cleverly accentuated by the tiers of narrow windows on either street.

PLATE ELEVEN
CHARTRES CATHEDRAL (about 1913)
Collection Mrs. L. B. Wescott, Clinton, N. J. 35¾″ x 19½′

IT IS NOT ASTONISHING that many French painters, as well as numerous artists from other countries, have made pilgrimages to the city of Chartres, in northern France, in order to sketch or paint its gorgeous Cathedral of Notre-Dame. This thirteenth-century church, built on a hill overlooking the valley of the Eure, is famous for its stained glass windows, and for its two unequal spires, the older, shorter one plain and symmetrical, the other one richly adorned with late Gothic decorations. A medieval

chronicler called this House of God "the very couch and chamber of Our Lady." More recently, the American historian, Henry Adams, in his book, *Mont Saint-Michel and Chartres,* remarked about the Cathedral of Notre-Dame: "Like all great churches that are not mere storehouses of theology, Chartres expressed, besides whatever else it meant, an emotion, the deepest man ever felt—the struggle of his own littleness to grasp the infinite."

A devout Catholic, Utrillo viewed this wonderful Gothic edifice in a spirit of humility matching, if not surpassing, that of the Protestant and rationalist Adams. He worked with a patience and meticulousness reminiscent of the old masters, and thus gave to his painting of the cathedral the sense of stability and durability for which one will look in vain in the Impressionists' glimmering paintings of churches. This imposing canvas was done about 1913 when, at the age of thirty, Utrillo had reached the height of his "white period." The dainty signature in the lower left corner, incidentally, is not by the master himself. Annoyed with Utrillo's huge and ugly handwriting of this period, his dealer, Libaude, usually asked the artist's mother to sign for him.

PLATE TWELVE
THE PHILOSOPHER'S TOWER (about 1917)
Museum of Fine Arts, Boston. 15″ x 21¼″

THIS PICTURE HAS ON ITS BACK an inscription in the artist's handwriting listing the subjects on view—the Philosopher's Tower, the old Bray farm, the Moulin de la Galette, and, in the distance, the church of Sacré-Coeur. Here Utrillo painted with a lighter hand and dipped more frequently into bright colors than in his "white period," which ended about 1914. Gone is the weightiness and severity of earlier years, and there is, instead, a poetic looseness of handling, a lucidity and transparency reminiscent of Japanese landscapes of the mid-nineteenth century. It is hard to believe that this serene masterpiece was painted in a grim period when Utrillo, having exhausted himself in drinking bouts, sought help in one mental hospital after another.

PLATE THIRTEEN
THE BERLIOZ HOUSE AND THE HUNTING LODGE OF HENRY IV (about 1917)
The Art Gallery of Toronto, Canada. 21¼″ x 28¾″

THE MODEST LITTLE HOUSE seen in the lower left corner is one which Utrillo painted from several different angles. The house was located on the corner of two picturesque Montmartre streets, Rue du Mont-Cenis and Rue Saint-Vincent. It was inhabited between 1834 and 1837 by young Hector Berlioz and his English-born wife in the first years of their romantic marriage. Here Berlioz eked out a bare existence by grinding out articles on musical affairs for newspapers. Here his only child, Louis, was born, and here he wrote his famous second symphony, *Harold in Italy* (inspired by Lord Byron), a comic opera, *Benvenuto Cellini,* and sketches for one of his greatest and most famous works, the *Grande Messe des Morts (Requiem),* commissioned by the French government in memory of those who died in the July revolution of 1830.

Tradition has it that somewhere in this neighborhood stood a hunting lodge owned by the sixteenth-century French king, Henry IV. Allegedly, the king stayed there during the first siege of Paris, and there wooed the lovely abbess of the Convent of the Sisters of Saint-Denis. "Paris resisted, but the lady fell," a historian wittily remarked.

After the First World War, both houses were razed, and the district of Montmartre was covered with large, modern residences. Whatever the importance of this picture as a historical document may be, we regard it as a calm and muted symphony, linking together the leaden sky, the white walls, the red roofs, and the intertwining foliage of winter trees.

5

PLATE FOURTEEN
STREET SCENE (about 1925)
Museum of Fine Arts, Boston. 9½" x 6¼"

NOTWITHSTANDING HIS GROWING FAME as an artist, Utrillo in 1924 was in such a state of despondency that he tried to end his life by beating his head against the wall of the cell to which he had been brought after an alcoholic spree. Removed by his mother from the temptations of Paris and safely installed in a chateau near Lyons, he recovered rapidly and was soon painting some of his finest canvases. It was at this time that he painted *Street Scene* from his memory of Montmartre. The melancholy, bordering on morbidity, of earlier days is gone. Instead, the colors are rich and gay, and, for once, people appear as recognizable human beings, not as mere color specks. But unlike his friend Modigliani who drew the Parisian women as slender, sensitive beauties, Utrillo saw them only as large-hipped, plump fishwives. His interest in women seems to have been reserved for such big, fleshy types.

PLATE FIFTEEN
SACRE-COEUR DE MONTMARTRE AND
PASSAGE COTTIN (1934)
Collection William P. Seligman, New York. 24⅞" x 18¾"

WHEN UTRILLO, ALREADY PAST FIFTY, painted this scene, he did so either from memory or from a picture postcard. He no longer lived in Montmartre and was hardly ever allowed to visit it. The tourist, walking with Utrillo eastward along the Passage Cottin, ascends some steps to reach the Rue Chevalier de la Barre which leads directly to the basilica of Sacré-Coeur.

Painted in gouache—opaque water color prepared with gum—this picture is a product of Utrillo's "colorist period." Here the white is dominant only because this scene represents winter. Generally, the pictures produced after 1920 abound in gay and bright colors such as are rare among the Utrillos of the "white period." Everything is daintier, more meticulously drawn, but the over-all effect is weaker. The dynamic force that drove the young, unreformed artist is almost gone. Typical of this period are the people who are no longer mere specks of color. One notices how often the figures in Utrillo's paintings are moving away from the spectator, suggesting an effect of loneliness and isolation.

PLATE SIXTEEN
FLOWER STILL LIFE (1946)
Collection Miss Lily Pons, New York. 36" x 28"

SUZANNE VALADON, WHOSE FORTE was the nude, painted a few strong and sturdy flower still lifes. As for her son, time and again he turned away from his beloved houses to depict flowers in pots or vases. He was not always successful with this subject, and he did not paint it frequently; nevertheless, he has done enough flower pieces so that a Paris gallery, in the summer of 1951, could adorn all its wall space with works in this genre.

Undoubtedly the shy Utrillo prefers flowers to people. They do not upset his balance by endless talk, they can be taken up, arranged, and discarded at will. Unlike the Impressionists before him, he does not care to wrap his flowers in a glowing, vibrating light. From Cézanne—who even used artificial flowers as models—Utrillo learned how to rescue painted flowers from the atmospheric mists in which they sometimes became lost, and how to give them solid, healthy forms. With vehement, expressive brush strokes, Utrillo gives these calla lilies and hothouse carnations some of the melancholy overtones and artificiality of his street scenes.

The present work, painted when he was over sixty, is among the best he produced in this genre. During the war the singer Lily Pons gave unstintingly of her talent to aid France; when she re-visited the country, the Utrillos gave this flower still life to her as a present. The gift was accompanied by a letter, signed by the artist and his wife Lucie:

Here is the painting of flowers which we are happy to give you in homage to your magnificent talent and your great patriotism for the grand French cause.... May these flowers of France perfume your drawing-room and remind you of us.

THE TITLE, SIZE, AND OTHER PERTINENT DATA ON THE PAINTINGS THAT FOLLOW,

WILL BE FOUND BY LIFTING EACH REPRODUCTION

Maurice Utrillo. V.

Sacré-Cœur de Montmartre
et Passage Cottin —

Maurice, Utrillo, V,
1934,